Girls RESEARCH!

by Jennifer Phillips

Consultant:
Dr. Georgina M. Montgomery

Assistant Professor
Lyman Briggs College and the Department of History
Michigan State University
East Lansing, Michigan

CAPSTONE PRESS
a capstone imprint

Savvy Books are published by Capstone Press,
1710 Roe Crest Drive, North Mankato, Minnesota 56003
www.capstonepub.com

Library of Congress Cataloging-in-Publication Data
Phillips, Jennifer, 1962– author.
Girls research! : amazing tales of female scientists / by Jennifer Phillips.
pages cm. —(Savvy. Girls rock!)
Summary: "Through narrative stories, explores female scientists who have made major contributions in science and culture"—Provided by publisher.
Includes bibliographical references and index.
ISBN 978-1-4765-4056-6 (library binding) — ISBN 978-1-4765-6162-2 (ebook pdf)
1. Women scientists—Biography—Juvenile literature. 2. Women in science—Juvenile literature. I. Title.
Q130.P527 2014
509.2'2—dc23
[B]   2013035450

Editorial Credits
Jennifer Besel, editor; Lori Bye and Bobbie Nuytten, designers; Svetlana Zhurkin, media researcher;
    Laura Manthe, production specialist

Photo Credits
AIP Emilio Segre Visual Archives, Physics Today Collection, 25 (bottom); AP: dapd, 11; Capstone Press, cover (silhouette); CDC, 31; Colorado State University, Department of Public Relations, 27; Columbia University, 29; Corbis: AP/Irwin Fedriansyah, 10 (bottom), Bettmann, 45 (top), 52 (left), National Geographic Society/Mark Thiessen, 17 (top); Courtesy of the Lemelson-MIT Program and Michael Branscom Photography, 56 (top); DVIC, 55; ESA/Hubble & NASA/N. Rose, 28 (top); Eskind Biomedical Library Special Collections/VUMC, 48, 49; Getty Images: Express Newspapers, 16 (top), Gianni Tortoli, 44 (bottom), Jemal Countess, 56 (bottom), Popular Science/John B. Carnett, 21, Science Source, 50, Theo Wargo, 6; Glessner House Museum, Chicago, IL, 42; Library of Congress, 7, 8, 9, 13, 22, 23, 24 (bottom), 40 (all), 57 (top), 59; NASA, 36 (top and bottom), 37 (top and bottom), GSFC, 18 (top); National Cancer Institute, 12, 52 (right); National Library of Medicine, 34; Newscom: akg-images, 57 (bottom), akg-images/Doris Poklekowski, 53 (right), EPA/Matthew Cavanaugh, 47 (bottom), EPA/Uwe Anspach, 47 (top), Everett Collection/CSU Archives, 10 (top), Getty Images/AFP/Paul Erlich, 19 (bottom), Gorka Lejarcegi, 53 (left), IP3/MAXPPP/Christophe Morin, 30, SIPA/Olycom, 60, UPI Photo Service/Roger L. Wollenberg, 32 (top), ZUMA Press/Marlene Awaad, 14 (middle), ZUMA Press/The Washington Times, 28 (left); NOAA: OAR/NURP, 20; Photo by Brett Hobson, 19 (top left); Photo by David von Becker, 39; Photo by Rick Potts, 44 (top); Rensselaer Polytechnic Institute/Hart, 5; Shutterstock: Alex Landa, 35, alphaspirit, 16 (bottom), Anna Frajtova, 58–59, Archiwiz, 1 (top left), Binkski, 17 (bottom), Davor Ratkovic (splatter), 42, djem, 23 (back), Dzianis Hluboki, 4–5 (bottom), Igor Kisselev, 54, 55 (back), Jose Antonio Perez, 36–37 (back), Juli Hansen (DNA), 52–53, knikola, 33 (top and bottom), 61, Liubov Mikhaylova, 10–11 (border), 48–49 (back), Milos Dizajn, 8–9, mw2st, cover (background), N_ZHM, 6 (back), Nella, 7 (back), 40–41, Ohmega1982, 14 (bottom), Oleg Iatsun, 14 (frame), Omelchenko, 12–13 (back), Petr Vaclavek (arrows), 36, 37, Raj Creationzs, 32 (bottom), rangizzz, 6 (frame), rubikscubefreak, 28 (back), Rui Manuel Teles Gomes, 19 (top right), Sashkin, 46 (bottom right), schab, 44–45 (border), secondcorner, 14–15 (back), Sergey Nivens, 46–47 (back), Transia Design (waves), 20, 21, Valerio Pardi, 24–25 (back), Varvara Gorbash, 2–3, 56–57 (back), wawritto, 51, willmetts, 26–27 (back), wongwean, 1 (bottom), 62–63, 64; U.S. Fish and Wildlife Service/National Digital Library, 18 (bottom); Washington University in St. Louis/Department of Anthropology, 45 (bottom); WHO: Pierre Albouy, 33; Wikipedia: Gerbil, 46 (bottom left)

Direct quotations are placed within quotation marks and appear on the following pages. Other pieces written in first-person point of view are works of creative nonfiction by the author.
p4: rpi.edu/president/profile.html; p11: www.people.com/people/archive/article/0,,20119362,00.html; p12: www.achievement.org/autodoc/page/eli0int-6; p15: www.reuters.com/article/2013/01/10/bbva-climate-award-idUSnPnDA40851+160+PRN20130110; p17: www.pbs.org/wgbh/nova/secretlife/scientists/mireya-mayor/; p20: www.nytimes.com/1991/06/23/magazine/champion-of-the-deep.html?pagewanted=all&src=pm; p26: www.npr.org/templates/story/story.php?storyId=5165123; p28: news.discovery.com/space/always-a-bridesmaid-vera-rubin-and-the-nobel-prize.htm; p29: discovermagazine.com/2010/jul-aug/20-the-dark-hunter#.Ug0zgKV5jTQ; p30: www.scienceheroes.com/index.php?option=com_content&view=article&id=393&Itemid=357; p32: marketingforscientists.tumblr.com/post/1316049532/famous-women-scientists-an-interview-with-former-nsf; p33: www.youtube.com/watch?v=G-FCL4I2dLU; p35: www.nytimes.com/1994/01/30/magazine/joycelyn-elders.html?pagewanted=all&src=pm; p39: discovermagazine.com/2002/nov/feat50#.Uh48P6V5jTT; p46: www.nytimes.com/2007/07/03/science/03conv.html?pagewanted=all&_r=3&; p60: www.nytimes.com/2012/12/31/science/dr-rita-levi-montalcini-a-revolutionary-in-the-study-of-the-brain-dies-at-103.html?_r=0

Printed in the United States of America in Brainerd, Minnesota.
092013 007770BANGS14

BLAZING A TRAIL

Women have been scientists and inventors for a very long time. But the road to discovery hasn't been easy.

THEY HAD TO FIGHT TO GO TO SCHOOL.

For years society said women didn't need to be educated.

THEY HAD TO FIGHT FOR JOBS.

For years society said women should not work outside the home.

THEY HAD TO FIGHT FOR RESPECT.

For years society said women weren't smart enough to make major contributions.

But women busted through these barriers. A brave group of women blazed the trail for new generations. They developed thick skin and pursued science with curiosity, courage, and determination.

Medical cures, discoveries about ancient civilizations, new species, revelations about the size of the universe ... the list of accomplishments marches on. What a different world this would be if female scientists hadn't persevered.

Shirley Ann Jackson

August 5, 1949–

In 2005 *Time* magazine called Shirley Ann Jackson "perhaps the ultimate role model for women in science."

In 2007 the National Science Board called Jackson "a national treasure."

Extraordinary praise for an extraordinary scientist.

Jackson is among the United States' foremost leaders in science education, research, and public policy. She has held leadership roles in universities, corporations, and the U.S. government. She is a powerful leader, powerful speaker, and a powerful supporter of science.

In 1973 Jackson became the first African-American woman to receive her doctorate degree in physics from the Massachusetts Institute of Technology (MIT). But her list of accomplishments did not stop there.

- President Bill Clinton appointed Jackson to serve as chairman of the U.S. Nuclear Regulatory Commission (NRC). As the leader of the NRC, she led the group to keep nuclear energy safe in the United States. Jackson was the first woman and the first African-American to serve as NRC chairman.

- The National Women's Hall of Fame inducted Jackson for her work in science, education, and public policy.

- The American Association for the Advancement of Science (AAAS) elected Jackson to serve as the group's president. The AAAS is the world's largest general scientific society.

- President Barack Obama appointed Jackson to the President's Council of Advisors on Science and Technology. The group's job is to advise the president on ways to use science to strengthen the economy.

Extraordinary praise for an extraordinary scientist.

5

EDNA FOA

1937–

I was born in Haifa, Israel. While I've had many happy times in my life, I've also faced sorrow and pain.

My older brother was killed as a soldier during the Arab-Israel war of 1948. It was a terrible blow to my family. Four years later, my father died of a heart attack. Then, as an adult, I saw firsthand the terrible effects of combat during the Palestinian uprisings in my country.

Perhaps these events shaped the direction of my work as a psychiatrist.

I study and treat anxiety disorders. I want to help people with obsessive-compulsive disorder, post traumatic stress disorder, and social phobias become healthier and less afraid.

In the 1980s I started believing patients could overcome their traumatic memories, fears, and anxieties by confronting them. In 2000 I developed a prolonged exposure approach to use with people who suffered traumas. With this treatment I guide people in imagining and describing the bad thing that happened. Or, if it is possible and safe, I have them go out and do things in the real world that help them take control of their fears.

Some people considered this treatment very radical. But this therapy method has now helped heal many people, including soldiers and victims of war, terrorism, and natural disasters.

I'm called an innovator and an expert in my work. I'm just proud to be helping so many people. And when I get recognition for my work, I see it as a chance to get the word out. I want people to know there are treatments that can help.

Anna Freud

December 3, 1895–October 9, 1982

I was born in Austria to a very famous father. Imagine being the child of Dr. Sigmund Freud, the "father of psychoanalysis." I was surrounded by his many books, and the flow of people in and out of his consulting room. He even treated me as a patient while I was a young woman.

I suppose it's no big surprise that I too became a psychiatrist. But I didn't just follow in my father's footsteps. I made my own contributions in the mental health field.

My work began in the 1940s during World War II. I started working with the British government to create safe havens for children made homeless by the war. The country was under attack, with bombings a regular danger. I helped my young patients learn to cope with the trauma of war and poverty.

I began pioneering new methods for child therapy. I helped adults see that children's environments influenced their ability to cope with stress and suffering. And my research revealed how children actually develop in stages. They grow from being very dependent on others to being self-reliant.

I was certainly swimming against the tide. People believed then that children's behavior was unpredictable. I wrote and taught about how these stages shaped children's health and behavior. Growing up was more predictable than we realized.

My efforts made child psychology an acceptable practice. This knowledge is used to help children around the world work through their troubles.

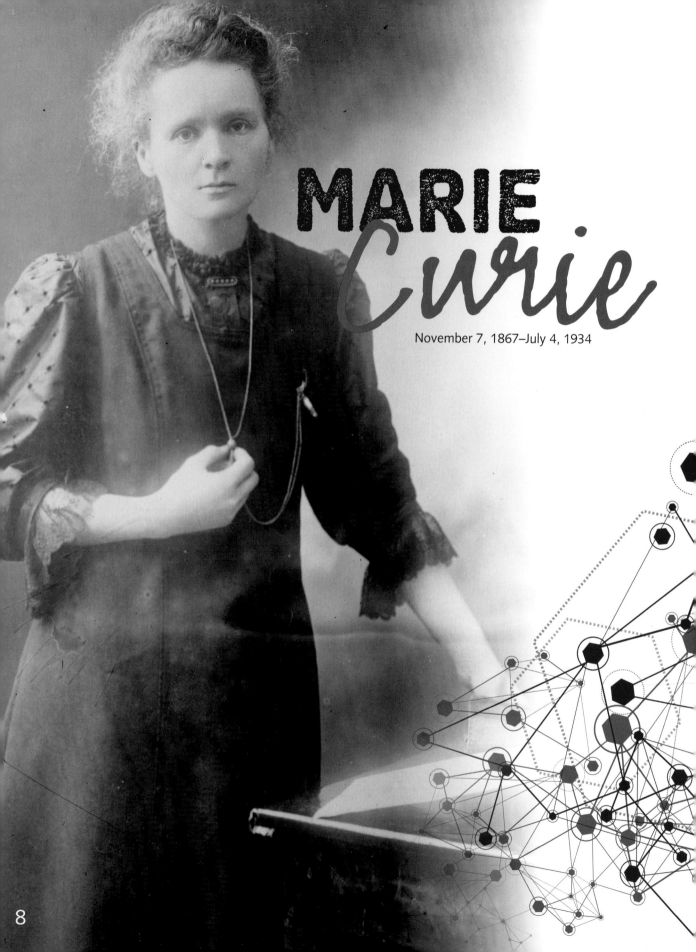

MARIE
Curie
November 7, 1867–July 4, 1934

A teeny tiny speck. One-tenth of a gram. That's what Marie Curie and her husband, Pierre, found after three years of toiling. But it was enough for her to keep looking. And what she found would change the world.

Over and over, Curie dissolved huge chunks of minerals in chemicals. The minerals and chemicals created a thick sludge. She manipulated the sludge to try to find tiny levels of radioactivity, where atoms break apart and create energy.

The work paid off. In 1898 Curie, a physicist-chemist, discovered a radioactive element she named polonium. Four years later she discovered what became known as radium. Curie's discovery of these rare and precious elements introduced a very powerful natural source of heat and light.

Her research also changed some deeply held scientific beliefs. Before her discoveries scientists thought atoms were the smallest pieces of matter. Curie's findings taught scientists about the particles that make up atoms. Research took off in new directions, including the development of nuclear energy, treatment of diseases such as cancer, and military uses.

Curie became the first woman to win a Nobel Prize for science. Later she became the first woman to win two Nobel Prizes. Tragically, the very discoveries that helped others hurt her. Years of handling radioactive materials ravaged her body. Curie died from a disease caused by long exposure to radiation.

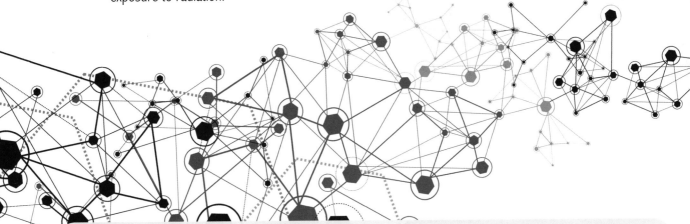

LIKE Mother, LIKE Daughter

Irène Joliot-Curie (September 12, 1897–March 17, 1956) certainly didn't have an ordinary childhood. By age 17 she was joining her mother, Marie Curie, in the lab. She earned her own Nobel Prize for creating artificial radioactivity. The invention meant radioactive atoms could be created faster and cheaper than extracting natural radium, the technique her parents developed. Having artificial radioactivity allowed quicker development of nuclear energy, weapons, and medical treatments.

Joliot-Curie (right) with her husband Frédéric

9

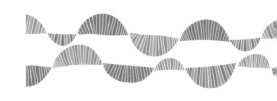

MONKEYING AROUND

These groundbreaking researchers have spent countless hours deep in the jungles, watching the behaviors of primates. What they discovered changed the world's understanding of these amazing creatures.

Jane Goodall

April 3, 1934—

Jane Goodall is a world-renown primatologist and influential environmentalist. She spent five decades conducting research about chimpanzees in Tanzania. Her research revealed that chimps have humanlike behaviors, such as forming relationships and using tools.

Biruté Mary Galdikas

May 10, 1946—

Biruté Mary Galdikas has spent more than 30 years in the jungles of Indonesian Borneo becoming a world expert on orangutans. Orangutans prefer to be alone, so collecting information on them is difficult. But Galdikas patiently introduced herself into the environment and slowly came to discover what these creatures' lives are like.

Dian Fossey

January 16, 1932–December 26, 1985

Dian Fossey forever changed science's view of gorillas. She collected extensive details during her 20 years of research in the mountains of Africa. Before her work, gorillas were seen as frightening beasts. But Fossey revealed how social, curious, and affectionate gorillas can be.

She published the book *Gorillas in the Mist.* This book spread awareness about protections needed to keep gorillas in the wild. But not everyone agreed with Fossey. She was murdered at her research camp in 1985. The killers have never been caught.

"I think all three of us put together will help us better understand our own place in nature—that we're not as different from the animal kingdom as we think."

—Jane Goodall, speaking about how she, Galdikas, and Fossey became known as the "trimate" for their connected studies of primates

GERTRUDE ELION

January 23, 1918–February 21, 1999

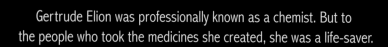

Gertrude Elion was professionally known as a chemist. But to the people who took the medicines she created, she was a life-saver.

Elion's inventions have helped people who are fighting cancer, AIDS, kidney disease, and other medical problems. In her lifetime she accumulated 45 medical patents, 23 honorary degrees, and a Nobel Prize. And she revolutionized how drugs are developed.

"I think I'm most proud of the fact that so many of the drugs have really been useful in saving lives. I've run into people whose lives have been saved ... I run into people who have had kidney transplants for 20 years who are still taking the drug. And I don't think anything else that happens to you can match that type of satisfaction."

ELION AND WRIGHT THROUGH THE YEARS

1949
Wright becomes one of the first scientists to test chemotherapy medicine on human cancer cells. Later, she creates a way to test anticancer drugs on tumors to identify which ones work best for a patient's cancer.

1959
Elion receives a patent for the first major medicine to fight leukemia.

1962
Elion gets a patent for her medicine that allows people unrelated to kidney patients to donate an organ.

1950

1960

JANE COOKE WRIGHT

November 20, 1919–February 19, 2013

Starting in the 1950s, Jane Cooke Wright began her groundbreaking research on chemotherapy. The result was proven drug therapies that get medicines directly to tumors, boosting the success of cancer treatment.

Wright meticulously constructed her research studies. She carefully cataloged data so she could analyze how different dosages and methods worked. Along the way she became an influential advocate for better cancer care. She helped establish a professional society focused on studying the treatments given to cancer patients. She also accepted a presidential appointment to establish a national network of treatment centers.

Others held her up as an example of progress for women and minorities. She preferred to stay focused on just making a difference with her science.

1964
Wright develops a non-surgical way to deliver potent drugs to tumors deep within the body. She also helps found the American Society of Clinical Oncology.

1967
By this year Wright's role as head of the chemotherapy department and associate dean at New York Medical College made her the highest ranking African-American woman in a U.S. medical institution.

1983
Elion helps develop the first AIDS drug, AZT.

1988
Elion is awarded the Nobel Prize in Medicine.

1970

Susan Solomon

January 19, 1956–

Many people dream of saving the planet. But Susan Solomon is actually trying to do it. The atmospheric chemist has spent an extraordinary amount of time working to counteract damage to the ozone layer. This layer protects Earth from harmful radiation.

Solomon's research has put her in the coldest places on the planet. She has worked for months at a time in near-constant darkness and sub-zero weather in Antarctica and the North Pole. In these harsh settings, she measured atmospheric molecules for evidence of ozone-depleting chemicals.

By the 1980s chlorofluorocarbons (CFCs) were used in everything from hair spray bottles to refrigerators. These chemicals were used to propel products from cans and to cool things down. But Solomon proved that CFCs were depleting the ozone layer. Her research contributed to a global ban on this chemical.

Solomon's awards are numerous. She has a National Medal of Science. She worked with former U.S. Vice President Al Gore and was awarded a Nobel Prize. *Time* magazine named her one of the most influential people in the world. And she won the 2012 Vetlesen Prize, the top award given for earth sciences research.

And if all that isn't enough, Solomon has an Antarctic glacier named in her honor.

"My discovery really increases the importance of making good choices about how much more carbon dioxide we want to put into the atmosphere, because we need to understand that what we are doing cannot be easily undone."

Joy Adamson

January 20, 1910–January 3, 1980

When Joy Adamson's husband, George, came home one day in 1956, he had a surprise. George was a game warden in the Shaba Game Preserve in Kenya, Africa. He had been forced to shoot a lioness in self defense. And now he needed to find a way to care for the lioness' three newborn lions.

Adamson swooped into action. This was life on the plains of Kenya. But she couldn't have imagined how her story would bring wildlife conservation and research to the world stage.

The runt of the litter deeply bonded with Adamson. Named Elsa, this little lion would suck on Adamson's thumb and playfully stalk members of the human "pride." The Adamsons encouraged Elsa's wild nature and prepared her to return to the wilds of Kenya. Their work paid off.

Afterward, Adamson wrote a book about Elsa's journey. *Born Free* became a bestseller. Then the book was turned into a bestselling movie. All the attention helped the Adamsons raise money for conservation and wildlife education. Adamson created the Elsa Wild Animal Appeal Fund and helped establish the World Wildlife Fund.

But her work didn't stop with Elsa. Adamson published stories about bringing up Pippa, a young cheetah, and Penny, a leopard cub, for release back into the wild.

Adamson's long-time love of Africa and its wildlife spurred a fire of passion worldwide to save African animals.

MIREYA MAYOR

September 6, 1973–

It was a sweltering night in the jungles of Madagascar. Mireya Mayor and her research team had finally found the object of their expedition. The mouse lemur fit in the palm of her hand.

Mayor kept the tiny creature in her tent until morning. Then she and her team conducted their tests. The tests confirmed what Mayor already knew. This adorable animal was a newly discovered species.

For Mayor, an anthropologist and primatologist, it was another successful project. Since the age of 23, she has been all over the world studying wildlife and advocating for habitat protections. She also works as a wildlife journalist for many TV programs. She travels across the planet to discover the beauty of animals and help save them from extinction.

KEEP YOUR OPTIONS OPEN

Mayor started her professional life as an NFL cheerleader. While always interested in animals, it was a college class in anthropology that hooked her on studying primates and shifted her to a science career.

"You can love cheerleading or art or whatever it is and you can still be

SAVING THE PLANET

RACHEL CARSON

May 27, 1907–April 14, 1964

Rachel Carson couldn't help herself. She had to write. Often late into the night after her day job as a marine biologist, she wrote lyrical prose inspired by her nature research. At work, she convinced her U.S. Fish and Wildlife Service supervisors to let her write and edit public booklets about conservation.

Her combined love of writing and the environment changed the country. Carson made environmental science a public discussion and concern with her book *Silent Spring*. The book raised alarms about the harmful effects of pesticides used in agriculture. Carson became the focus for both praise and criticism. Farmers and chemical companies challenged her data and accused her of exaggerating the problem. Confident in her research findings, she weathered the attacks. Because of Carson's work, some pesticides were banned and more controls on their use were put in place.

TIERNEY THYS

December 31, 1966—

Marine biologist Tierney Thys absolutely adores the Mola mola. And she wants others to share her love for this giant ocean sunfish. She tracks and studies the odd-looking mola's behaviors (including their big appetite for jellyfish). She also collects details about other ocean life, including how climate change affects animals. Thys is a pro at combining research with media attention to influence people to change harmful practices. She helped persuade eBay, for example, to ban the trading of invasive species. Look for her on networks such as National Geographic, Nature, and PBS. She likes to take viewers into her oceanic world to educate and inspire everyday environmentalists.

GRETCHEN DAILY

October 19, 1964—

Ecologist Gretchen Daily has been tackling tough issues since she was a teen. Daily researched acid rain and industrial pollution. From there, she was off and running as a budding scientist.

Daily is now working with companies and countries that say saving the environment is too costly. She helped invent computer software that shows where healthy environmental practices make good financial sense. The software assists governments in deciding how to fund green initiatives.

Sylvia Earle

August 30, 1935–

The suit made her look like part astronaut and part machine, but it kept Sylvia Earle from being crushed in the ocean. Deeper and deeper she sank until she touched bottom. She was 1,250 feet (381 meters) below the surface. Then she walked. She walked the ocean floor, spotting the glowing creatures in the pitch-black environment. She touched plants that shot out rings of blue fire. For 2½ hours, Earle walked—without a tether—on the ocean floor. It was 1979. Earle's journey was a courageous, record-breaking, daring expedition. And she is the only person to ever do it.

What Earle found on the seafloor strengthened her desire to explore and protect Earth's oceans. It's a scientific mission she's been leading for more than five decades. The ocean is less mysterious and its role on the planet more valued because of her.

"People are under the impression that the planet is fully explored, that we've been to all the forests and climbed all the mountains. But in fact many of the forests have yet to be seen for the first time. They just happen to be underwater. We're still explorers. Perhaps the greatest era is just beginning."

Earle (left) showing sea life to another aquanaut

- She has been diving since the age of 17.

- Earle is the former chief scientist of the National Oceanic and Atmospheric Administration (NOAA).

- She is one of first pilots to take a one-person submersible vessel to a depth of 3,000 feet (914 m).

- In 1970 Earle, leading a team of female aquanauts, lived in an undersea habitat for two weeks.

- She has been deemed a Living Legend by the Library of Congress.

- Earle has spent more than 7,000 hours underwater.

- She has led more than 70 undersea expeditions.

- *Time* magazine designated her a "Hero for the Planet."

- *The New Yorker* and *The New York Times* called Earle "Her Deepness."

- Earle is an oceanographer, explorer, author, and lecturer.

LISE MEITNER

November 7, 1878–October 27, 1968

ALBERT EINSTEIN compared her to the brilliant Marie Curie. Others called her the mother of nuclear power.

In 1938 Lise Meitner explained how an atom splits. She called this event nuclear fission. But it was a bittersweet accomplishment for the experienced physicist. She realized her discovery of nuclear fission meant the introduction of a tremendous energy source that could be used for right or wrong. During World War II, governments raced to create atomic bombs using this new science. Her fears coming true, Meitner refused to be involved.

But her discovery also led to good. It led to the creation of nuclear reactors that produce electricity. And it helped future scientists better understand how atoms work.

Meitner was given very little credit for her discovery. In 1944 her long-time research partner, Otto Hahn, won the Nobel Prize for his work with nuclear fission. Meitner had given Hahn the critical data he needed for his work. But she did not receive part of the prize.

Today scientists recognize Meitner for her major contributions.

Chien-Shiung Wu

May 31, 1912–February 16, 1997

Newspapers called her "the atom smasher."

Chien-Shiung Wu had found a way to separate two types of uranium atoms, a key step for producing uranium fuel. Understanding how to produce this forceful energy earned her a spot on the secretive team working on the Manhattan Project. This team was charged with building atomic bombs for the United States during World War II.

Wu became known as a world expert in nuclear fission techniques. She proved a new theory about beta decay, a type of radioactivity. She identified how fast electrons come out of an atom's nucleus when the atom is stabilizing itself. She also helped reverse a common belief that particles are symmetrical, with both sides behaving the same. She proved that this parity law doesn't always hold true, forcing scientists to rethink how the universe developed.

Some scientists felt Wu was wrongly excluded from a Nobel Prize related to the parity law discovery. But she didn't let such slights stop her passion.

Maria Mitchell

August 1, 1818–June 28, 1889

Maria Mitchell's accomplishments were as bright as the stars she loved to watch.

By age 14 Mitchell was helping whaling boat crews complete the navigational computations that guided their voyages.

At age 17 she opened her own school to train girls in math and science.

At age 29 Mitchell discovered a comet using a simple 2-inch (5-centimeter) telescope. This discovery was an American scientific first. She was soon elected to be the first woman in the American Academy of Arts and Sciences.

By age 31 she was working as the first professional female astronomer, earning $300 a year. She calculated the positions of planets and helped develop the growing science of weather forecasting.

Henrietta Leavitt

July 4, 1868–December 12, 1921

Henrietta Leavitt wanted to work as an astronomer. But women in the late 1800s still weren't considered scientists. Leavitt volunteered for seven years at the Harvard College Observatory. Finally, the Observatory started paying her for the work she'd been doing for free.

Leavitt created a way for astronomers to measure the distance from Earth to any visible pulsating star in the universe. With her discovery scientists were able to begin mapping the universe.

She discovered more than 2,400 stars that change brightness.

She also invented a way to make photographic measurements of stars, called the Harvard Standard.

Deaf most of her life, Leavitt was a quiet, humble rebel. She gently nudged her way forward in the profession she loved. Modern-day astronomers say her contributions are still helping with new discoveries today.

"I was watching cattle go through a squeeze chute for their vaccinations. It's a device they put the cattle in to hold them still. And I noticed that some of the cattle just kind of relaxed. So I went and tried out the squeeze chute. And the pressure calmed me down. Many individuals with autism find that deep pressure applied over large areas of the body has a very, very calming effect on the nervous system. So then I built a squeezing machine that I could get into that worked with an air cylinder and an air compressor where I could work a little control handle and I could squeeze myself. And I used that to calm down."

Temple Grandin

August 29, 1947–

Temple Grandin has been changing views about autism, a condition that makes it difficult to understand social cues. And she's been using autism to change views about animals.

As an animal sciences professor, Grandin teaches ranchers and livestock handlers how to treat animals humanely. She's learned that animals, much like autistic people, think in pictures, smells, and touch. Animals can easily feel overwhelmed by smells, noise, and changes in routines. To improve livestock handling, she's designed corrals to decrease sensory overload. And she encourages the use of touch and pressure stimulation to help animals stay calm.

Her voice is just as prominent when it comes to helping people understand what it's like to be autistic. Grandin uses her personal experiences living with autism to make a difference in research, treatment, and society's understanding of the condition.

TimeLine

1947—Temple Grandin is born.

1949—She is diagnosed with autism.

1951—Grandin starts talking at age 4.

1965—As a teen Grandin invents the "hug" machine to help with autism treatment.

1970—Grandin earns a bachelor's degree in psychology.

1975—She earns her master's degree in animal science.

1980s—Grandin begins sharing her personal story to educate others about autism.

1989—She earns her doctorate in animal science.

2006—Grandin is featured on the BBC TV special "The Woman Who Thinks Like a Cow."

2010—A movie about Grandin's life is released. The movie is based on Grandin's books *Emergence* and *Thinking in Pictures*.

Grandin is also named one of *Time* magazine's 100 most influential people.

VERA RUBIN

July 23, 1928–

Vera Rubin started studying the skies with a telescope made from a cardboard tube. Technology replaced cardboard as she grew up. But curiosity continued to drive her exploration of the universe. And thanks to her scrutiny, scientists now know there's a vital element in the universe that can't be seen or touched.

Dark matter is an invisible material in galaxies. Rubin is the astronomer who confirmed that this unseen stuff actually exists.

Before the 1970s astronomers believed galaxy edges had less mass, which would mean a weaker gravitational pull. But Rubin discovered the opposite is true. And in doing so she found dark matter. Rubin measured the gravitational pull and orbiting speed of outer stars within galaxies. She found that a type of invisible mass existed. This invisible mass allowed outer stars to orbit at higher speeds than thought possible.

Rubin, with the help of other scientists, studied more than 200 galaxies. She came to believe that possibly 90 percent of the universe is made of dark matter. Rubin's discovery changed astronomy forever. She proved that what you can see is not all there is to find.

"Fame is fleeting. My numbers mean more to me than my name. If astronomers are still using my data years from now, that's my greatest compliment."

Elena Aprile

March 12, 1954–

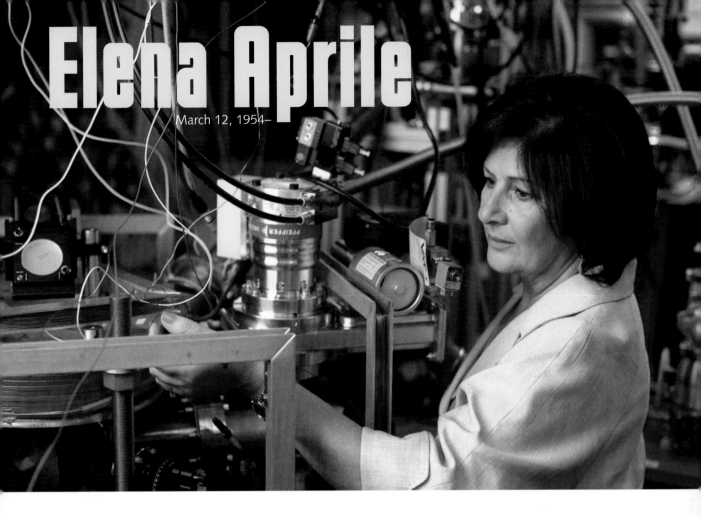

Elena Aprile spends her time deep underground working as a detective. She's building on the work of scientists such as Vera Rubin. While they know dark matter exists, they haven't yet seen it in any way.

Aprile, an astrophysicist, is trying to pick up dark matter movement.

Her lab is 5,000 feet (1,524 m) underground in Italy. Stainless steel containers filled with a dense substance called liquid xenon dominate the room. Highly sensitive cameras surround the containers, waiting to snap a shot of bluish light.

Aprile's equipment is trying to record signals that could only come from invisible particles called WIMPS. Scientists think dark matter comes from subatomic particles, or WIMPS, left over from the creation of the universe.

WIMPS are invisible because they don't reflect or absorb light. And they don't usually bump into atoms, which keeps scientists from feeling them.

Aprile's goal is to collide a WIMP with xenon atoms. She expects the evidence of a collision to be a bluish light and an electrical charge.

So far her experiments haven't recorded WIMP movement. But if one day she does, dark matter won't be so invisible any more.

"We must try and try again to find the truth. If we stop because there is no guarantee that we will find anything, then we would never find anything again."

"There is always hope in life, because there is always hope in science."

Françoise Barré-Sinoussi

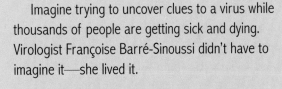

July 30, 1947–

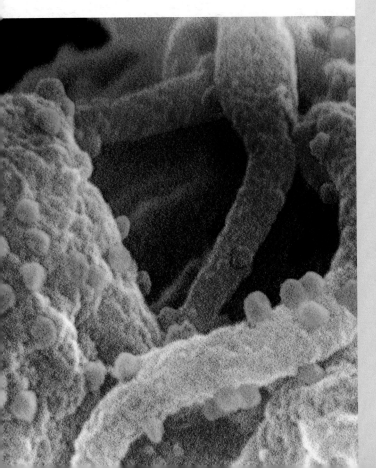

Imagine trying to uncover clues to a virus while thousands of people are getting sick and dying. Virologist Françoise Barré-Sinoussi didn't have to imagine it—she lived it.

Labs around the world were racing to find the cause for AIDS during the 1980s. It was in Barré-Sinoussi's French lab that answers started to emerge. She discovered the human immunodeficiency virus (HIV), the cause of the disease. This discovery allowed scientists to begin looking for ways to stop the virus.

Barré-Sinoussi's groundbreaking find led to a Nobel Prize in 2008. But she shrugs off individual recognition. Her team's success, she says, came from scientific teams collaborating with each other.

In fact helping patients and scientists in regions with limited resources has become as much her mission as wiping out AIDS. She helps link labs together to share information and spread research findings faster.

31

Rita Colwell

November 23, 1934–

It's not easy to convince people they're wrong.
But microbiologist Rita Colwell had to do just that.

"Do good science, and trust your data. If you're criticized by
other people, and if you believe your data, then stick by your guns
and trust your own instincts."

Before Colwell's groundbreaking work, scientists thought that
the deadly disease cholera could only be spread from person to
person. Cholera bacteria cause a person's body to release large
amounts of water in the form of severe diarrhea. If not treated
cholera can lead to a painful death. Scientists thought the bacteria
only spread through people's feces. If the bacteria in the feces
came in contact with a community's drinking water, many people
would get sick with cholera. But Colwell discovered that this isn't
the only way the bacteria spread.

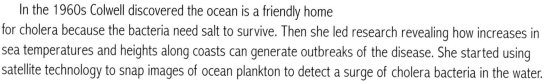

In the 1960s Colwell discovered the ocean is a friendly home
for cholera because the bacteria need salt to survive. Then she led research revealing how increases in
sea temperatures and heights along coasts can generate outbreaks of the disease. She started using
satellite technology to snap images of ocean plankton to detect a surge of cholera bacteria in the water.

Today Colwell studies how climates, community behaviors, and microorganisms connect. She's
on a mission to help countries and scientists from different fields unite to find solutions to wipe out
dangerous diseases.

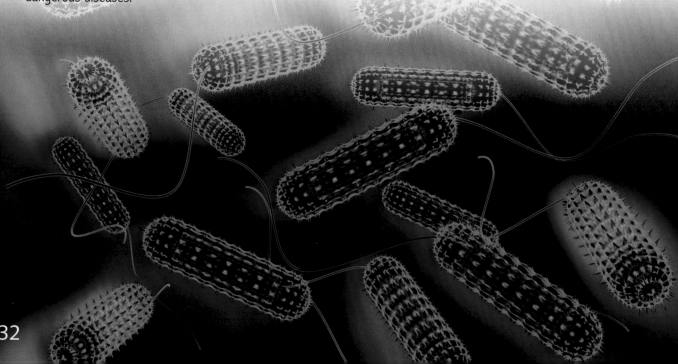

Margaret Chan

In 2013 *Forbes* magazine named her the 58th most powerful person in the world. Margaret Chan is the director of the World Health Organization. And she holds the health of the world in her hands.

Chan is a scientist who is charged with finding the best solutions to public health problems.

She is the only person who can say if a disease has become a worldwide pandemic. She makes recommendations on which medicines and treatments to use for diseases. She takes a stand against violence and dangers to children. And the world follows her advice.

"The people that are lost to road traffic accidents are normally young people. That is the price we have to pay. And we cannot afford to pay the price with young lives. It is entirely preventable, but it takes commitment, and it takes action, and it takes time. But we are running out of time. We must not let this be a missed opportunity. We know what to do."

—Chan speaking about the Long Short Walk campaign to make roads safer for pedestrians

World Health Organization

Joycelyn Elders

August 13, 1933—

People either loved or hated Joycelyn Elders.

In the 1980s and '90s Elders was a powerful voice for public health. She conducted research on how hormones affect children's bodies. She published more than 100 papers about growth problems and juvenile diabetes.

In 1987 then Governor Bill Clinton asked Elders to head the Arkansas Department of Health. In that role Elders convinced the state legislature to pass laws allowing lessons on substance abuse prevention and self-esteem in schools. She also pushed for lessons about sex education, a topic that made Elders unpopular with many people.

In 1993 President Clinton appointed Elders to the role of U.S. surgeon general. She became the first African-American, and only the second woman, to hold that post. But her time as Surgeon General was rocky. She continued to push her controversial beliefs. After 15 months in office, her opinions conflicted with the president's beliefs. She was asked to resign. Some said good riddance. Others said Elders had done a great deal to change the face of health care.

In an interview Elders said, "You've got to get people's attention before you can achieve change. As surgeon general, you have to take a stand. People are either going to love you or hate you."

STARS IN SPACE

These women haven't just proven they can fly high, fast, and far. They have excelled in the harshest environment there is—outer space.

ELLEN OCHOA
May 10, 1958–

- a NASA astronaut since 1990
- is the world's first Hispanic female astronaut
- was part of the crew that performed the first docking to the *International Space Station*
- became the director of the Johnson Space Center in 2013
- invented optical systems, including a system that inspected space objects, a system that identifies objects, and a system that made images taken in space clearer

hours spent in space: more than 978
number of space flights: 4

BONNIE DUNBAR
March 3, 1949–

- served as a NASA astronaut for 20 years
- served as payload commander during two missions, including a joint U.S.-Russian trip to the *Mir* space station
- helped design the thermal protection system used on the space shuttles

hours spent in space: more than 1,208
number of space flights: 5

MAE JEMISON

October 17, 1956–

- conducted experiments on the effects of weightlessness on bone cells while in space
- is the first African-American female astronaut
- was a medical doctor before becoming an astronaut

hours spent in space: more than 190
number of space flights: 1

KALPANA CHAWLA

July 1, 1961–February 1, 2003

- was the first Indian-born female astronaut
- served as mission specialist and robotic arm operator on the Shuttle *Columbia*
- upon re-entry of the *STS-107 Columbia*, the shuttle broke apart, killing Chawla and the other six crew members

hours spent in space: more than 734
number of space flights: 2

Ingrid Daubechies

August 17, 1954–

You've most likely never heard of **Ingrid Daubechies**. And her work is probably just as unknown. But her discoveries have changed the world in so many ways, it's getting hard to keep track.

Daubechies is a physicist and a mathematician. You also could call her the mother of wavelets. Daubechies developed the theory of wavelets. Wavelets are mathematical functions that are used to compress images into a smaller size. A wavelet-compressed image is smaller than a typical JPEG image. And if images are smaller, a computer or database can support more of them.

It's easy to see how wavelets change how people store data. But here are just a couple ways wavelets are already changing some businesses:

The FBI began uses wavelets with its fingerprint records. The organization predicted that using wavelets would reduce the amount of needed computer memory by 93 percent.

Medical offices have begun using wavelet technology with imaging systems such as MRIs. Because wavelets squeeze down the size of these huge files, pictures can be shared throughout a medical system.

"If you painted a picture with a sky, clouds, trees, and flowers, you would use a different size brush depending on the size of the features. Wavelets are like those brushes."

39

Elizabeth Blackwell

February 3, 1821–May 31, 1910

Florence Nightingale

May 12, 1820–August 13, 1910

My Friend Florence

One of my dearest friends was Miss Florence Nightingale. Many an hour we spent discussing the problems we saw with medical care.

I owe my awakening to the importance of hospital sanitation to my friend. This is a cause we took on together in the United States and in England.

Florence made nursing a noble and well-run profession. It took grit. She showed up in 1854 at an army hospital during the Crimean War. She and her team of nurses got the cold shoulder. Doctors didn't want their help. In true character Florence took one look at the awful conditions and got to work anyway. She spent long days getting better sanitation and healthier food in place to help the soldiers heal.

People back in Great Britain donated money to help the "Nightingale nurses" at the war front. And when she came home, they embraced her ideas about creating a nursing profession. She was able to start her own nursing school.

My friend was very determined and very persuasive. She used her statistics and writing skills to create reports and display data in tables and charts. These convinced people that dirty hospital conditions were unacceptable.

The modern field of nursing remembers Florence for her hard work establishing reforms. I think she would be pleased to know how her efforts paid off. Millions of highly trained nurses are working throughout the world today. And scientists have taken her early work on sanitation to a level she never could have imagined.

Elizabeth Blackwell

My Friend Elizabeth

My friend Elizabeth Blackwell wanted to be a doctor. She didn't have an easy time of it, that's for sure. It was the 1840s. Women weren't considered suitable to be physicians. But I learned quickly that Elizabeth didn't take no for an answer.

School after school rejected her. But she eventually got her medical degree. That made her the first female physician in the United States. But no one wanted to hire her. Not one to be stopped, she eventually opened her own hospital in New York.

I was stationed across the ocean in England, busy training nurses and doing my research about how dirty hospital conditions bred infection. We saw each other when Elizabeth traveled in England, and we kept in touch through letters.

There were things Elizabeth and I did not agree on, but improving conditions in hospitals was one passion we shared. We planned how to train doctors and nurses to wash their hands and keep clinical areas clean. It took a lot of work and patience. But we finally started making a dent in hospital sanitation.

Elizabeth's fingerprints are all over advances in modern medicine. More than anything I want her to be remembered for how she helped others.

Florence Nightingale

FRANCES GLESSNER LEE

March 25, 1878–January 27, 1962

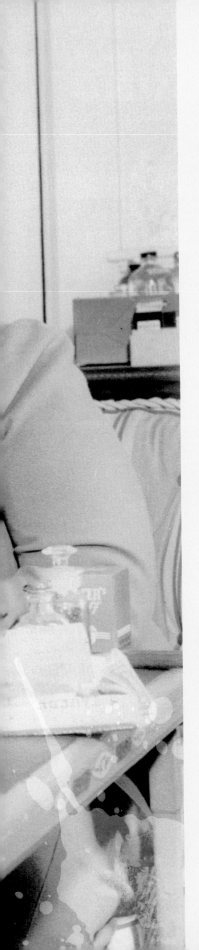

Frances Glessner Lee was proper and rich. She loved needlework and making dollhouses. She was also extremely frustrated. Wealthy women were expected to spend their days keeping a well-run home. But Glessner Lee wanted a career. Being creative and determined, she found a way to get one. In fact she created an entirely new profession—the field of forensic science.

You've probably heard of the TV show *CSI: Crime Scene Investigation*. In that show scientists study crime scenes to find out who committed a murder. That show isn't always accurate, but it does give people a glimpse into the real world of forensic science. Real scientists study blood spatter, collect fingerprints, and study details in a room. Many of the techniques forensic scientists use today were created by Glessner Lee.

Glessner Lee revolutionized crime scene investigation. In 1931 she started the Department of Legal Medicine at Harvard University. It was the first forensic science program in North America.

Then Glessner Lee combined her love of dollhouses with her passion for investigation. She created 18 miniature death scene dioramas she called the Nutshell Studies of Unexplained Death. Each scene featured a crime scene, complete with intricate details. Calendars on the wall included all the months. Blood spatter and other clues were placed with precision. Each diorama cost about the same as a regular-sized house. But their value in training was priceless. The models were used for years to train thousands of law enforcement professionals in investigation techniques.

SKELETON STORIES

These incredible scientists dug into the past to make their discoveries.

ANNA "KAY" BEHRENSMEYER
August 14, 1946–

Behrensmeyer is famous for pioneering a research method called taphonomy. This method helps her and other scientists study how organic remains become fossilized. Her approach allows scientists to learn what an environment was like when the fossilized animals or plants were alive.

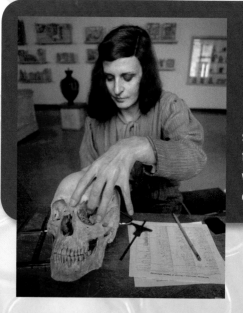

SARA BISEL
May 13, 1932–February 4, 1996

Bisel pioneered a technique to do chemical and physical analysis of skeletons. She extracted bone samples from chemical baths and studied them with lab equipment. The results gave clues about what people ate and what chemicals they encountered. This technique for examining skeletons can help tell a story about lifestyles, jobs, and dangers people faced.

MARY LEAKEY

February 6, 1913–December 9, 1996

Leakey was dedicated to exploring Africa's Rift Valley. There she discovered early human fossils, such as skulls and footprints. Those fossils revealed that humans had been on Earth a lot longer than previously believed. The fossils also showed that early humans were more like apes, but that they walked upright and were more advanced with tools than expected.

PATTY JO WATSON

1932–

Watson spent four decades crawling through cool, dark caves. She uncovered prehistoric artifacts and clues to how early humans lived. Her research yielded a treasure trove of information about early farming and how caves were used for mining, burials, housing, spiritual rites, and more. Watson also invented new floatation techniques to retrieve small, delicate artifacts. Using water or other solutions, she showed how to carefully separate heavier and lighter fossilized plants from other materials.

Elizabeth BLACKBURN

November 26, 1948–

The cellular biologist documented findings in her handwritten notes. She experimented relentlessly with different techniques. What was so consuming? Elizabeth Blackburn had discovered strange sequences at the ends of the microscopic chromosomes that carry genes and help cells grow. These telomeres weren't repeating themselves in a sequence based on what scientists knew about DNA. And she wanted to know why.

Blackburn spent years learning all she could about telomeres.

Her resolve paid off. In 1984 she found the enzyme that creates the tiny telomeres. This enzyme gave Blackburn the answer she sought. The telomeres can look different because they wear down as people age or because of diseases such as cancer.

"Telomeres are the protective caps at the ends of chromosomes in cells," she says. "Chromosomes carry the genetic information. Telomeres are buffers. They are like the tips of shoelaces. If you lose the tips, the ends start fraying."

Blackburn's work also suggested there could be ways to slow or reverse some of this deterioration. Now there's research happening to see if vaccinations can wipe out the telomere enzyme levels that create cancer cells. Maybe someday Blackburn's discovery will lead to cures for the world's deadliest diseases.

FROM STUDENT TO NOBEL COLLEAGUE

Molecular biologist Carol Greider was a graduate student who helped Blackburn complete her research on telomeres. Talk about a career starter! Greider shared in the Nobel Prize that resulted from their work. She now runs her own lab where she continues working on how to stop or reverse damage to telomeres.

As a child Greider suffered from dyslexia. She was put in remedial classes, had a hard time in school, and thought she was stupid. To overcome her disability, Greider became very good at memorizing things. This turned out to be a great skill for science.

Carol Greider
April 15, 1961–

47

Food &

The MyPlate nutrition guide is a handy tool to help people eat healthy. But MyPlate wasn't the first dietary guideline. Interest in creating dietary recommendations for U.S. citizens started in the 1940s. Wars and economic depressions had taken their toll on people's health. Scientists studying diseases had discovered that good nutrition was key to good health.

Governments around the world began researching nutrients and how much of them people needed. And women were at the forefront of this research. In fact 25 of the 43 scientists who worked on the first U.S. Recommended Dietary Allowances (RDAs) were women. Two women in particular played significant roles in developing the regulations for healthy eating—Hazel Stiebeling and Lydia Roberts.

Hazel Stiebeling

1896–1989

Growing up as a farm girl during the early 1900s went hand in hand with interest in food and nutrition for Hazel Stiebeling.

By college she was hooked on chemistry. She conducted research on how bodies absorb vitamins and change food into fuel. After she finished college, the U.S. Department of Agriculture beckoned with a chance to lead a new department focused on food economics. Stiebeling leaped at the opportunity.

Soon she was designing nutritious but inexpensive diets to help low-income families. She also created nutrition guidelines she called "dietary allowances."

Stiebeling was a perfect fit when the government wanted to organize a committee to develop the first scientifically based recommended dietary allowances (RDAs). Stiebeling became a critical contributor, helping establish the language of RDAs that is still used today.

Nutrition

Lydia J. Roberts

June 30, 1879–May 28, 1965

Lydia Jane Roberts had a passion for teaching and a passion for science. Combining those loves led to an extraordinary career as a nutrition scientist.

Learning about malnutrition became Roberts' specialty. She spent much time in the field, visiting and living in different places to learn from families about their food habits and environment.

Working with local agencies, she combated hunger with practical, lasting solutions. She pushed for families to have electricity to refrigerate food. She taught people to have home gardens, chickens, and small farm animals. She advocated for healthy meals to be served at school.

The White House regularly called on Roberts to serve on committees studying children's health issues. When the government wanted to develop a new set of recommended dietary allowances, it tapped Roberts to lead the charge.

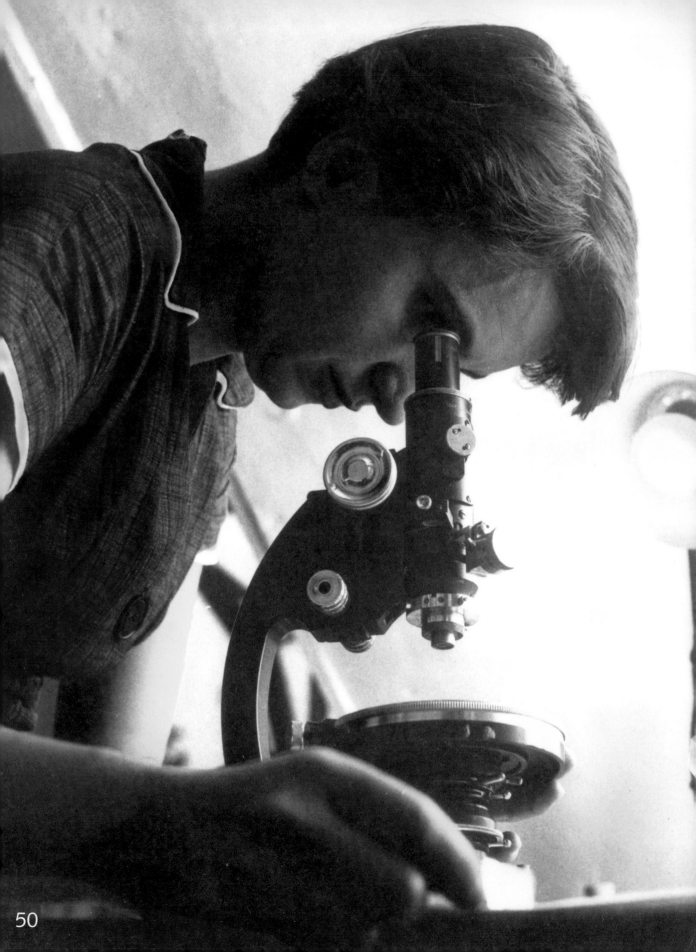

ROSALIND FRANKLIN

July 25, 1920—April 16, 1958

Rosalind Franklin's story is rarely told. Her work is rarely praised. But her photo—simply called photo 51—was the key to discovering the structure of DNA.

It was the 1950s. Franklin had already become an expert in using X-rays to create images of solids. In fact she was the pioneer in using this method to analyze molecules. When she was hired by King's College in London to study living cells, she felt she had earned her place.

But another scientist at the college, Maurice Wilkins, disagreed. He felt that Franklin was his assistant. Their relationship was strained from the start. But Franklin continued her groundbreaking work. She learned how to produce a very fine beam of X-rays that would allow her to take pictures of finer fibers of DNA than ever before. One photo in particular changed everything. Photo 51 actually showed the cellular structure of DNA.

But before Franklin could share her discovery, Wilkins shared the photo with two other scientists at Cambridge University. In 1953 Wilkins and the other two scientists published their proposed structure of DNA. They failed to mention that much of their proof came from Franklin's photo.

Franklin never received an award for her DNA discovery. But the world now knows how important her research was.

It's ALL in

If you look anything like your mom or dad, you can see how traits are passed from generation to generation. But for decades scientists wondered how those traits were passed on and why. These incredible researchers made great strides in answering those questions.

Barbara McClintock

June 16, 1902–September 2, 1992

1950s—Barbara McClintock learns that genes can turn physical characteristics, such as height or hair color, on or off. This idea is known as jumping genes.

Maxine Singer

February 15, 1931–

1960s—Maxine Singer figures out how to "read" genetic code.

1980s—Singer finds that a type of gene can jump around in DNA, providing clues into the causes of genetic diseases.

the Genes

Christiane Nüsslein-Volhard
October 20, 1942-

1980s—Christiane Nüsslein-Volhard uncovers how single-celled embryos become complex living animals.

Mary-Claire King
February 27, 1946-

1970s— Mary-Claire King discovers that chimpanzees and humans are genetically 98 percent the same.

1990s—King proves that breast cancer is inherited in some families.

GRACE HOPPER

December 9, 1906–January 1, 1992

I didn't set out to change the world. I just had a good idea that I believed in. And I wanted others to believe in it too. My idea was simple—make computers easier to use. Actually doing that was a bit more difficult.

I was always a math whiz. When I joined the Navy during World War II, I was sent to work on a computation project at Harvard. I worked on some of the earliest computers—big things that filled rooms and took specialists to program and use. The computers were used to make mathematical tables. They weren't at all useful for everyday tasks. But I saw the potential.

I started working on a new computer that was more user-friendly. Instead of putting in numbers to tell the computer what to do, why couldn't we use English words? I created compilers that allowed people to make programs with words instead of complicated strings of numbers.

Getting people to believe in my idea wasn't easy though. I had to give speeches—sometimes up to 200 a year—to audiences throughout the country. Eventually, people started to see that computers could be used for all kinds of businesses.

I just knew computers could make our lives easier. Now anyone can use them.

010110111010111001000010000101010111011100 11
101111010111110101110000101010101 00101
0011111100000101101011000101000010101111001101001 11
0111010000010101011001010100110101010010101100 10
101100100100010101001010100110100101010101011 01
1000001100111101010010101010101010101001011011000101000101101 00
101010011010101010101100101000101011101010100010101011110101000 01
1101110101010001010101000101010110100001010101110101010001010
101000100001000010000100010000100001000010000100010000100001000101100100110 01
0101110101111010011110101110001111101001111100011111000111110101111100110010011110101 1
0101011101010010100111001010101010101011110101110100011000000010000100010000010000010000 0
0101101110101110010000100001010101110111001100110101010001011001 11
101111010111110101110000101010101001010010001011001010001 00
0011111100000101101011000101000010101110011010011101101010 1
011101000001010101100101010011010101001101010101110101011010100011000 100
1011001001000101010010101001101001010101010110100100010001000100100100100010001 0
100000110011110101001010101010101010100101101100010100010110100001010001000100010010 0
1010100110101010101011001010001010111010101000101010111101010001001000101111010111100111 1
101010101010001010100010100010101011010001010101110101010001010111001111010111001111010 1

Inspiring Inventors

Women rock the world of inventing too. From products that save lives to methods that make modern technology possible, these scientists have inspired the world.

Stephanie Kwolek

July 31, 1923—

Stephanie Kwolek invented a family of synthetic fibers now used around the world. Kwolek's patented fiber inventions, such as Kevlar, Lycra, and Spandex, are stronger but lighter than steel, and they don't rust or corrode. Her fibers are used to make bulletproof vests, boats, airplanes, ropes, cables, tires, skis, tennis rackets, protective gloves, fiber optics, and more.

Patricia Bath

November 4, 1942—

Patricia Bath was the first to do many things. She was the first African-American to finish a residency program in ophthalmology. But she's best known for her invention. Bath created a device that uses a laser to treat cataracts. In 1986 she became the first African-American female doctor to receive a patent for a medical invention.

Katharine Burr Blodgett

January 10, 1898–October 12, 1979

Look out a window today, and you don't even think about the glass. You can thank Katharine Burr Blodgett for the "invisibility" allowing you to see clearly. Glass wasn't always that clear. Before Blodgett, glass looked distorted because light traveled through it. Blodgett figured out how to add a thin coating to glass that reflected 99 percent of the light hitting it.

Hedy Lamarr

November 9, 1913–January 19, 2000

Hedy Lamarr was a glamorous actress during the 1930s, '40s, and '50s. But she was also an inventor. Working with a partner, Lamarr patented a torpedo guidance system during World War II that used frequency hopping. This hopping method repeatedly switched radio frequencies used to launch missiles. The constant switching helped missiles avoid being intercepted or jammed. Her idea wasn't used during the war, but it is today. Lamarr's idea became an early stepping stone in creating what is now modern-day WiFi.

Virginia Apgar

June 7, 1909—August 7, 1974

Virginia Apgar's name is said in every delivery room in every corner of the world. Her name has become one of the most well-known medical assessments ever created.

While working in delivery rooms, Apgar noticed babies didn't get much attention right after birth. The focus was on the mothers. But infant survival rates weren't great. Apgar believed assessing newborns on a few basic health vitals right away could improve their chances. These assessment items eventually became a system using the letters of her name:

A Appearance: Look at the baby's skin color

P Pulse: Is the baby's heart rate too high or too low?

G Grimace: Check the child's reflexes.

A Activity: Does the child have good muscle tone?

R Respiration: Is the baby having trouble breathing?

Anyone born after the mid-1950s has probably directly benefited from Apgar's assessment tool. Doctors and nurses began evaluating infants right away. With this early attention, many problems were discovered and treated quickly.

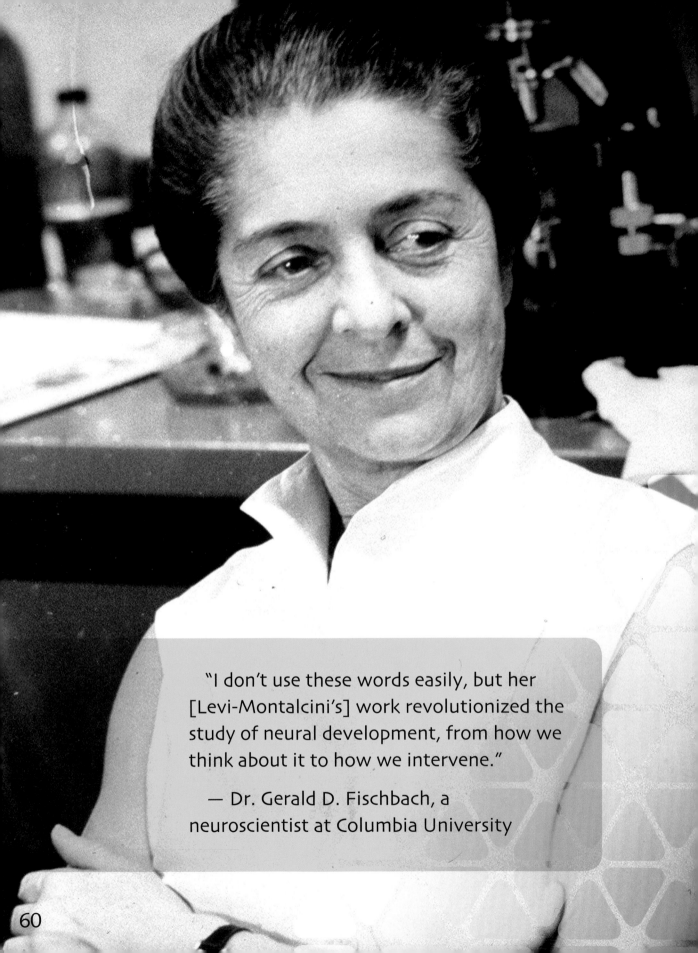

"I don't use these words easily, but her [Levi-Montalcini's] work revolutionized the study of neural development, from how we think about it to how we intervene."

— Dr. Gerald D. Fischbach, a neuroscientist at Columbia University

Rita Levi-Montalcini

April 22, 1909–December 30, 2012

When neuroscientist Rita Levi-Montalcini was 77 years old, she won a Nobel Prize. When she was 100, she was still showing up for work.

Call her strong-willed, but Levi-Montalcini didn't like to take no for an answer. She became a doctor even though her father forbid her from attending college. She did her research in hiding when Italian dictator Benito Mussolini ordered that Jews like her could not have professions. And she ignored society's ideas about women needing to marry.

Dubbed the "Lady of the Cells," Levi-Montalcini became known as one of the top brain scientists in the world. She discovered a key chemical protein that bodies use to grow cells and develop nerve networks. She called her discovery a "nerve growth factor."

Her discovery is still fueling medical research today. Now that scientists know the proteins exist, they can study what goes wrong with them.

NO LIMITS

Women explore every nook and cranny of our world, from the depths of the ocean to the boundaries of space. They introduce inventions that improve and save our lives. They help us understand our past and drive us into the future.

Their stories inspire all who hear them to work harder,

push farther,

and dream bigger.

THEY PROVE THAT NOTHING IS IMPOSSIBLE FOR

GIRLS WHO ROCK

Many of these women researched and explored over several decades.
Their placement on the timeline reflects the decade in which they truly made history.

1840s:

Maria Mitchell

1850s:

Florence Nightingale

1860s:

Elizabeth Blackwell

1900s:

Henrietta Leavitt

Marie Curie

1930s:

Hazel Stiebeling

Katharine Burr Blodgett

Lise Meitner

Lydia J. Roberts

1940s:

Anna Freud

Chien-Shiung Wu

Frances Glessner Lee

Hedy Lamarr

1950s:

Barbara McClintock

Grace Hopper

Rita Levi-Montalcini

Rosalind Franklin

Virginia Apgar

1960s:

Gertrude Elion

Jane Cooke Wright

Jane Goodall

Joy Adamson

Mary Leakey

Maxine Singer

Rachel Carson

Rita Colwell

Stephanie Kwolek

1970s:

Biruté Mary Galdikas

Mary-Claire King

Patty Jo Watson

Sylvia Earle

Vera Rubin

1980s:

Anna Behrensmeyer

Carol Greider

Christiane Nüsslein-Volhard

Dian Fossey

Elizabeth Blackburn

Françoise Barré-Sinoussi

Ingrid Daubechies

Patricia Bath

Sara Bisel

Susan Solomon

Temple Grandin

1990s:

Bonnie Dunbar

Ellen Ochoa

Joycelyn Elders

Kalpana Chawla

Mae Jemison

Margaret Chan

Shirley Ann Jackson

2000s:

Edna Foa

Gretchen Daily

Mireya Mayor

Tierney Thys

2010s:

Elena Aprile

INDEX

Read More

McCann, Michelle Roehm and Amelie Welden. *Girls Who Rocked the World: Heroines from Joan of Arc to Mother Teresa.* New York: Alladin, 2012.

Tougas, Shelley. *Girls Rule! Amazing Tales of Female Leaders.* Girls Rock! North Mankato, Minn.: Capstone Press, 2014.